MUSHROOMS and TOADSTOOLS

The deadly
Death Cap

OTTO
GREGORY

Illustrated by Sheila Bewley

FREDERICK MULLER

First published in Great Britain in 1972 by
Frederick Muller Limited, Fleet Street, London E.C.4

Printed in England by Ebenezer Baylis & Son Ltd, Leicester
and bound by William Brendon, Tiptree

SBN: 584 62038 1

Contents

MUSHROOMS AND TOADSTOOLS

If you walk in the woods in autumn you will find growing in grass, or among dead leaves around trees, or sprouting from mossy glades, several kinds of queer, soft, pale little plants which are quite unlike the green plants we all know. In almost any thick wood you can find some of these among the undergrowth, especially in warm weather after a few days of rain.

Some kinds of these little plants also grow in fields and meadows, or along hedges. Others grow on tree-trunks, or on stumps of old trees which have fallen and died.

Small as they are, they are much the largest of a very big and special group of plants which the botanists who study them call *fungi* (each single plant is called *a fungus*, and each kind *a species*).

Fungi grow all over the world, and there are thousands of different kinds — some 100,000 species altogether — most of them much too small to see, except through a microscope.

In Britain, for instance, there are some 3,000 species which are large enough to see and admire as they grow in the fields and woods. Although they are most common in autumn, some of them can be found at all times of the year.

Most people in England believe that only one kind — the white-capped ones, pink or brown underneath, which not only grow wild, but are cultivated and sold by greengrocers — are good to eat. These we call 'mushrooms'. All the others are believed by most people to be poisonous and these are generally called, rather contemptuously, 'toadstools'.

As we shall see, this is wrong. Only a few of the 'toadstools' are dangerously poisonous. Many more are good to cook and eat (some of them very good) but it needs experience and study to know and to recognize the good ones. All the rest are harmless: neither good to eat nor poisonous; but always interesting and strange. They are often beautiful, too, and well worth collecting and studying; and they may be more correctly described as 'wild mushrooms'.

Plants – with a Difference

Fungi are plants, but they are different from other plants we know in the way they get their food, and in the kind of food they need. They are also different from nearly all other plants in the way their new young plants are produced.

All other plants (and trees are plants too) have, inside them, a green dye or colouring matter which is called *chlorophyll*. It is this which gives them their green leaves and stems.

Without it none of them could live, for it is this chlorophyll which enables the green plants to make their

own food. With its help they get energy — that is power — from the sunlight. They use their power to make the kind of food they need from the gas *carbon dioxide*, which is in the air, and from water.

Alone among the plants fungi have no green chlorophyll.

So they cannot make their own food.

They take, or you might say they steal, what they need to live and grow from other plants or animals, living or dead, or from the remains of these.

The other way in which fungi are different from all other plants except the ferns, mosses, lichens, and sea-weeds — the way in which new, young fungi are produced — is due to the fact that fungi have no flowers or seeds.

All the other plants have flowers. From these flowers the seeds are grown, and from these seeds new plants can grow.

Seeds are like eggs. They have the beginning of a new plant — an embryo — inside them, as well as a supply of food. The food is used to help the young new plant to begin to grow until it is big enough to feed itself.

The fungi have no flowers, and so no seeds.

Instead of seeds they produce tiny cells called *spores*, and it is from these spores, if everything is right, that the new fungi will grow.

The spores are tiny, no more than specks of dust, so

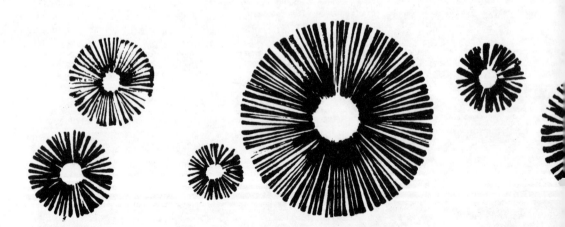

small that they can only be seen under a microscope or when thousands of them fall on one spot and make a little heap of dust. (There is a way, as we shall see later, in which you can make a little heap of spores for yourself and see the dust.)

When the time comes, the tiny spores are shot off from the parent fungus and fall to the ground. Or they are blown about by the wind to fall eventually, perhaps a long way from their first home.

Because they are so tiny they can carry no food or nourishment inside them as the seeds of the flowering plants do.

So, unless they chance to fall just where the very kind of food they need is lying they are certain to die.

But the chances of any one little spore finding exactly what it needs to live are millions to one!

Luckily, however, each single one of the mushrooms or toadstools growing in the woods or fields may produce millions of these tiny spores. So, among them all, one or two stand a chance of falling where everything is just right and of growing into a new plant.

Or should we say: it is lucky that the spores are so difficult to please? For if they could grow just anywhere, with the millions of them there are, they would very soon cover the whole earth!

Gills, Tubes, Spines, and Spores

If you look underneath the cap of an ordinary field mushroom you will see a great many thin, narrow bands, like blades, radiating from the stem towards the edges of the cap. These are called the *gills*. On these gills the spores grow in enormous numbers—it has been calculated that a mushroom with a cap four inches wide may have 16,000 million spores! When the time comes they are shot off and perhaps one, or even two, may find all the conditions right and grow into a new plant.

Many of the different fungi have gills like the common mushroom and are called the 'gill fungi'. Others have, under the cap, instead of gills, a sponge-like mass of tiny tubes within which the spores grow. Others have

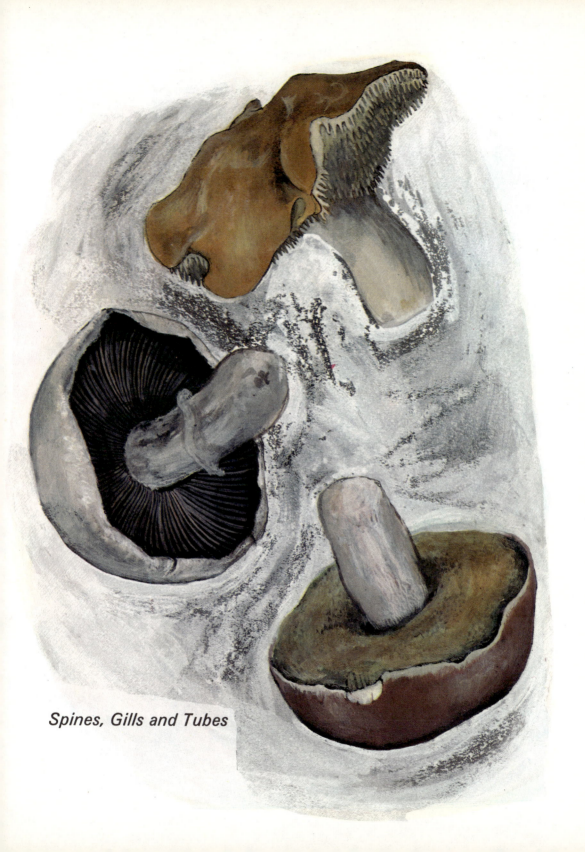

Spines, Gills and Tubes

little spines which carry the spores. In others, like the puff balls, the spores grow inside the fruit-body and this eventually bursts and sets them free.

The Mycelium

The mushroom or toadstool which we see growing above ground is not the most important part of the fungus plant.

The main part of the plant is underground. It is a web of tiny tubes, finer than hairs, though these may join together to form threads just big enough to be seen. This is the fungus spawn which botanists call the *mycelium*.

It is through these fine tubes that the plant is able to take in from its surroundings the nourishment it needs to grow.

Above ground many, but not all, of the fungi have the familiar, umbrella-like, mushroom shape with a round cap supported on a stem.

The purpose of the cap is to produce, and later shoot off, the spores from which some of the new fungi will grow. Since these spores are, for the fungus, what fruit is for a fruit-tree, the part above ground which we know as the 'mushroom' or 'toadstool' is called by botanists the *fruit-body*.

16

Poisonous, or Good to Eat ?

Although most people in Britain believe that only one kind of wild fungus is good to eat and that all the others, which they call 'toadstools' are poisonous, this is by no means true.

The one everybody knows to be good and likes to eat is the Field Mushroom. This has a white or creamy cap and pink or brown gills, and is very like its cousin, the cultivated mushroom which the greengrocers sell.

The fact is that many other kinds of wild mushroom can be cooked and eaten safely, and a number are very good.

Only a few species are poisonous and dangerous, but one or two of these are quite common. They grow in the same places as the good ones and are so deadly that it is a matter of life and death, if you are collecting for the kitchen, to know how to recognize each kind. Then, a few other kinds are good to eat cooked, but can cause illness if eaten raw.

There is no general or simple rule for telling which ones are good and which are not. The only way to know is to learn all about the shapes and colours of the different parts of each species — sometimes their special smell is important, too, and sometimes the colour of the spores, and even the size and shape of the tiny spores seen under the microscope.

However, there are some which are good to eat, not

difficult to recognize, and which cannot be mistaken for any dangerous ones.

Examples of these are given in the following pages, as well as details of the dangerous ones.

Seeing the Spores

Although each single spore is much too small to be seen without a microscope there is an easy way to collect a heap of them big enough to be seen.

Simply cut off the stem of a gill or tube fungus where it joins the cap and lay the cap, gills or tubes downwards, on a sheet of white paper. Cover the cap with an inverted glass jar (to prevent the spores from being blown away), and leave overnight.

By the morning thousands of spores will have dropped onto the paper and can be seen as dust, forming a pattern of the gills or tubes. This pattern is called a 'spore print'.

In this way it is possible to see the colour of the spores very clearly and this is sometimes useful in deciding to which species a fungus belongs.

There is another way to see the spores, while they are actually falling, after they have been shed from the cap.

For this experiment you need a glass tumbler or jar, an electric torch, and a full-grown gill or tube fungus (it must be full-grown so that the spores are ready to be shed).

Cut off the stem and place the fungus, gills or tubes down, over the mouth of the glass. Leave everything in complete darkness for an hour. Then shine the torch onto the glass and you will see the spores falling. Although the spores are themselves too small to be seen their movement can be seen by the light they reflect.

The Parts of a Fungus

In order to know what kind of fungus we have found we need to be able to recognize the different parts. This picture shows a cut through the centre of the poisonous Death Cap — a typical gill fungus — (A) when young, (B) full-grown.

The young fungus is completely covered by an un-broken skin called the *universal veil*. Inside this is a second skin, the *partial veil*, enclosing the cap and the gills, and attached below the gills to the stem.

A.

As the fungus grows both skins break. Small pieces of the universal veil often remain on the cap forming small warts. Part of the universal veil also remains at the base of the stem forming a sheath or cup called the *volva*. Parts of the partial veil remain on the stem forming the *ring*.

Not all species of the gill fungi have a ring or volva. So it helps towards recognizing a species to know whether or not it has these.

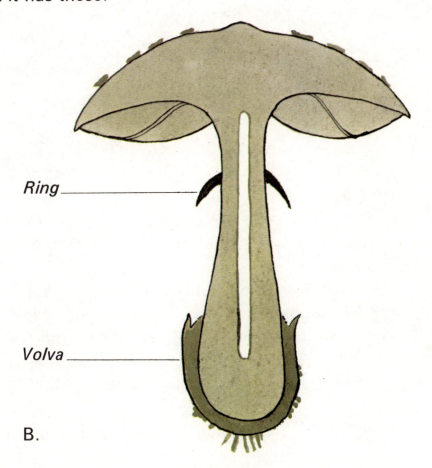

Ring_____

Volva_____

B.

Fairy Rings

In fields and meadows, and on grassy downs, we often come across circles of grass, darker and richer than the rest.

These are Fairy Rings and, in ancient times, they gave rise to many legends and fancies of nightly fairy revels.

Sometimes there are two rings, one within the other, with a ring of bare ground between. People used to think that this was worn bare by the nightly dancing of fairies.

There were other fanciful explanations and, in some

countries, the rings are still called 'Witches' Rings', but it is now known that these rings are caused by mushrooms and toadstools.

The fungus spawn, the mycelium, grows outwards in all directions if there is nothing in the way, and so forms a circle.

In taking what it needs for food it alters the make-up of the soil. One effect is to make the soil richer with the kind of chemical salts which the grass needs for nourishment. That is why there are rings of greener, richer grass.

When the right time of year comes, the mushrooms or toadstools sprout from the spawn and grow above ground. So we often find them growing in the shape of a ring.

Many different species form these Fairy Rings. One of the most common is called the Fairy Ring Champignon (the botanical name is *Marasmius oreades*). This can be found almost anywhere on grassy places, quite often on grassy lawns, from July to November. And it is good to cook and eat.

The Fairy Ring Champignon

SOME COMMON EDIBLE FUNGI

In the following pages are a few of the mushrooms and toadstools which are quite common in our fields and woods. The Latin botanical names are given in brackets. First the ones which are good to cook and eat.

The Field Mushroom (*Psalliota campestris*)
This is the well-known common mushroom which everybody likes to find in the fields and to bring home for breakfast. It is very like the cultivated mushroom sold in shops, but the wild variety has much more flavour.

The upper side of the cap has a white or creamy-white skin which peels easily. Underneath the cap are the gills, pink when young, becoming brown later.

The Field Mushroom is most common from August to early November, but it may appear as early as May.

It grows in meadows — especially where there are cattle — as well as in gardens, orchards, and parks.

When young, before the cap opens, it might be confused with the poisonous Death Cap (page 41). However, the Death Cap has white gills so, if you are collecting Field Mushrooms to eat, make sure that you pick only those with the cap open and the pink or brown gills clearly showing.

Field Mushroom
(height about 10cm.)

26

The Parasol Mushroom (*Lepiota procera*)

This is one of our largest mushrooms, sometimes growing 30 cm. high with a cap 20 cm. across.

When young, it is very like a drumstick. When full-grown, the chief parts to notice are the large scaly cap with a hump in the centre, the white gills, and the scaly stem which is tall and slender with a ring which can be moved.

The Parasol grows in pastures and in clearings in the woods from July to November. When not too old and tough it is very good to cook and eat.

The Blewit or **Blue Leg** (*Tricholoma personatum*)

The cap is grey to pale brown with a tinge of violet, smooth and shiny. The stem is short and thick, streaked with violet.

The Blewit grows in pastures and meadows in late autumn. It is good to eat and it is still sometimes sold in shops and markets in the Midlands.

A variety very like it, though more violet, with violet caps, gills, and stem is found in woods and is called the Wood Blewit. This is also good to eat.

The Chanterelle (*Cantherellus cibarius*)

The Chanterelle is shaped like a funnel or horn, or like an umbrella blown inside-out, with wavy edges. Cap, gills, and stem are all egg-yolk yellow. It smells rather like apricots.

It grows in woods in summer and autumn. It is difficult to confuse with any poisonous species and is very good to cook and eat though, as it is a little tough, it needs thorough cooking.

The Shaggy Ink Cap or Lawyer's Wig
(*Coprinus comatus*)

The cap is long and slender with white silky scales and really does look quite like the wigs which lawyers wear in court.

The gills are white when young, later pink, and become black with age. Then the edge of the cap curls outwards and, when it is full-grown, the edge of the cap dissolves into a black ink. This allows the spores above to fall to

the ground as they are shed and it goes on until the whole of the cap has dissolved and only the stem remains. There is a slight ring on the stem which often disappears.

The Shaggy Ink Cap grows in hedges and fields, by the roadside, in gardens, and especially on or near rubbish-heaps from June to November.

When young it is very good to cook and eat and it can hardly be confused with any of the dangerous fungi.

The Wood Hedgehog (*Hydnum repandum*)

This belongs to a group of fungi with 'teeth' or spines, on which the spores are formed, underneath the cap.

The cap is pale yellow-brown tinged with pink, and wavy at the edges. Underneath is a mass of spines, very like the spines of a rubber brush.

The Wood Hedgehog grows from August to November in mixed woods. It is good to eat but should be well boiled as it is rather tough.

Above: Truffle-hunting
Opposite: Wood Hedgehog

The Cep (*Boletus edulis*)

This is one of a large group of fungi — the Boleti — which have a spongy mass of tiny tubes under the cap instead of gills. The spores are formed inside these tubes and, when the time comes, they are shot downwards through the holes or pores at the ends of the tubes.

From above the Cep looks like a teashop bun, for the cap is brown, glistening, and domed. Underneath the cap, the spongy mass of tubes is white at first and later greenish yellow.

The stem is sturdy, and light brown with a network of white veins near the top.

When cooked it is very good to eat. In fact, most people have probably eaten it without knowing, for it is used, because of its fine 'mushroom' flavour, in most of the brands of tinned mushroom soup. It is also sold in delicatessen shops, dried, as a flavouring for stews.

It grows in woods, especially in beech woods, from late summer until November.

When young the Cep may be confused with another of the Boleti, the Bitter Boletus, as this also has white tubes when young. This is much too bitter to eat and can be avoided by tasting a tiny piece before cooking.

Another of the Boleti is somewhat poisonous and must be avoided. This is easy to recognize as the tubes are red, and they and the white flesh turn blue if they are bruised or broken.

The Oyster Mushroom
(*Pleurotus ostreatus*)

This is an example of the many fungi which grow on trees — especially on tree-trunks which are dead or dying.

The cap is smooth and shining, at first dark brown and then blue-grey. The gills are white and merge into a short stem. The cap is flattened and spreading; very like an oyster shell.

The Oyster Mushroom is most common in the autumn, but it can be found growing on tree-trunks, especially on beech trees, right through the year. It cannot be mistaken for any poisonous variety and is very good to eat when cooked.

The English Truffle (*Tuber aestivum*)

Truffles are small, irregular, potato-like fungi which are found just below the ground in woods. They are greatly prized by cooks for their delicate flavour and perfume and, being difficult to find, are almost worth their weight in gold!

The two kinds with the finest flavour grow in France and Italy and not in England. However, the English Truffle is also very good and has been collected commercially at least since the eighteenth century, until the last professional truffle-hunter retired in 1935.

Because truffles grow underground pigs and dogs with their keen sense of smell are trained to search for them in the woods. When the truffle is found, and the pig or dog begins to scratch it up, he is pulled away and rewarded with some other delicacy.

The English Truffle grows between 7 and 10 cm. underground and is found in beech woods and in chalky soil, especially in Wiltshire and on Salisbury Plain. Big ones sometimes crack the surface of the ground so it is just possible, with luck, to find them without a dog or pig to help.

(illustration on p. 32)

The Common Puff Ball (*Lycoperdon gemmatum*)
The Giant Puff Ball (*Lycoperdon gigantum*)

The Puff Balls belong to a group of fungi in which the spores are completely enclosed by the flesh of the fruit-body. When the spores are ripe the ball bursts and the spores are scattered by the wind.

The Common Puff Ball, a little smaller than a golf ball, is found mainly in woods in summer and autumn. It is whitish grey at first and later yellowish brown. The skin is covered with many small spines of different lengths. Below the ball is a short, stumpy stem.

When young it is completely white inside and at this stage is good to eat. Later, when the spores ripen, the inside is a mass of brownish spores and it can then no longer be eaten.

The Giant Puff Ball really is a giant, sometimes 30 cm. or more across. The outside of the ball is smooth and at first white, later becoming dull yellow.

At first, the flesh is also completely white and it is very good to eat, especially cut in slices and fried with the breakfast bacon. Later, when the spores develop, it is yellow inside and cannot then be eaten.

The Giant Puff Ball is found in pastures and woodlands in late summer and early autumn.

Common Puff Ball

Death Cap

PUBLIC ENEMIES! –
THE POISONOUS FUNGI

Although many people think that all 'toadstools' are poisonous there are, in fact, only a few which are dangerous and it is not difficult to learn what these look like.

However, these are so deadly, that nobody should ever eat any fungus unless he knows for certain what kind it is, and that it is a safe one.

The Death Cap (*Amanita phalloides*)

This is Public Enemy No. 1 – especially dangerous because it is deadly poisonous, quite common and, before the cap opens to show the white gills, may be mistaken for the common mushroom.

The colour of the cap varies from dirty white to yellowish green and is streaked, from the centre outwards, with dark fibres.

The gills and spores are white, there is a white or greenish-white ring on the stem, and the base of the stem is enclosed in the kind of sheath or cup which is called a 'volva'.

It is quite common in late summer and early autumn in woods, and in pastures near woods.

Two other poisonous fungi of the same *Amanita* species as the Death Cap and looking very like it are the

Fly Agaric and Red Staining Inocybe

Fool's Mushroom and the Destroying Angel. Their chief difference is that their caps are completely white. Luckily they are not very common. Yet another, also poisonous, is called the False Blusher. This is also like the Death Cap but its cap is dull brown with white warts.

The Fly Agaric (*Amanita muscaria*)

This is the toadstool of fairy-tales and often the model for nursery toys or painted stools. From its appearance nobody will be surprised to know that it is poisonous. It is called the Fly Agaric because, in some countries, it used to be broken up in milk, to attract and kill flies.

Although perhaps not deadly poisonous it certainly makes people very ill. It also affects the brain and causes a kind of intoxication. It is believed to have been used by the Vikings of Scandinavia to achieve the mad fury known as 'going berserk' and primitive tribes of Siberia have also used it to make themselves intoxicated.

Leaden Entoloma

It has a scarlet-orange cap with white warts. These are the remains of the skin which covered it when young and make it very easy to recognize. The gills and stem are white.

It is found from September to November, especially in pine or birch woods.

The Red Staining Inocybe (*Inocybe patouillardii*)

The cap of the Red Staining Inocybe is at first creamy white, then yellow, and later red, or brownish red. When young it turns red as soon as it is touched. The gills are at first whitish and later dull brown.

It is found in woods, especially in beech woods on chalky soil, from June to November; and it is dangerously poisonous.

The Leaden Entoloma (*Entoloma lividum*)

This has a greyish cap, sometimes with white patches. The gills are yellow at first and later pink, but they often remain yellow at the edges. The stem is pure white, often a little swollen at the base.

This fungus is found in the autumn, especially on grassy clearings in woods. It is poisonous enough to make people very ill and it has, occasionally, caused death.

These are the most dangerous or poisonous fungi which grow in Britain. However, among the 3,000-odd species there are a number of others which may cause

temporary illness and very many others which are too indigestible, or too tough, or too tasteless, or too nasty, to be eaten.

THE INVISIBLE FUNGI

The species we have described are just a few of the larger fungi. There are thousands of much smaller species — so small that they can only be seen under the microscope or when they are massed together.

These are the *moulds* and *mildews* which form on food which has been allowed to go bad, and may also grow on plants and on animal remains.

Other kinds of tiny fungi are called *rusts* and *smuts*, and some of these cause diseases in plants.

But not all of these minutely small fungi are harmful.

Some of them are valuable and very important in our lives.

One of them is yeast. Without yeast we could not bake our bread or brew our beer.

Another, the mould called *Penicillin*, is perhaps the most wonderful medicine we know, and has saved countless lives since it was discovered not many years ago.

So fungi are interesting in many different ways.

There are the mushrooms and toadstools of the fields and woods with their delicate shades of colour and varied and strange shapes. It is always a delight to find these, and interesting to collect them and find out which species they are by comparing them with the pictures in books. If you are expert enough to be quite sure which kind you have found, it is also very pleasant to cook the good ones and enjoy their different, and always savoury, flavours.

It is also exciting to remember the unimaginably small, yet varied, world of the tiny fungi: like their big brothers, sometimes harmful, but also often of great service to mankind.

Index